Water

Kay Davies
and
Wendy Oldfield

Starting Science

Books in the series

Animals
Electricity and Magnetism
Floating and Sinking
Food
Hot and Cold
Information Technology
Light
Local Ecology

Materials
Plants
The Senses
Skeletons and Movement
Sound and Music
Waste
Water
Weather

About this book

Water enables children to explore for themselves the different states that water exists in and the ways in which it behaves. They can test key concepts such as dissolving, absorbency, floating and sinking, and water pressure. They learn about the power of water to shape the land and its importance in maintaining life. Throughout, children will have opportunity to discuss and appreciate how water is part of our everyday lives.

This book provides an introduction to methods in scientific enquiry and recording. The activities and investigations are designed to be straightforward but fun, and flexible according to the abilities of the children.

The main picture and its commentary may be taken as an introduction to the topic or as a focal point for further discussion. Each chapter can form a basis for extended topic work.

Teachers will find that in using this book, they are reinforcing the other core subjects of language and mathematics. Through its topic approach *Water* covers aspects of the National Science Curriculum for key stage 1 (levels 1 to 3), for the following Attainment Targets: Exploration of science (AT 1), The variety of life (AT 2), Processes of life (AT 3), Types and uses of materials (AT 6), Earth and atmosphere (AT 9), Forces (AT 10) and Energy (AT 13).

First published in 1991 by
Wayland (Publishers) Ltd
61 Western Road, Hove
East Sussex, BN3 1JD, England

© Copyright 1991 Wayland (Publishers) Ltd

Typeset by Kalligraphic Design Ltd, Horley
Printed in Italy by
  Rotolito Lombarda S.p.A., Milan
Bound in Belgium by Casterman S.A.

British Library Cataloguing in Publication Data

Davies, Kay
Water. – (Starting science)
I. Title II. Oldfield, Wendy III. Series
  553.7

ISBN 0 7502 0206 8

Editor: Cally Chambers

CONTENTS

All the words that first appear in **bold** in the text are explained in the glossary.

Umbrellas go up when water falls from the sky as rain.
A rainy day can spoil our fun and stop our games.

RAINY DAYS

There is water all around us. It is even in the air we breathe. It collects in air as a **gas** called **water vapour**.

If the air high up in the sky becomes very cold, the water vapour changes into tiny drops of water.

This makes clouds.

When the drops get big enough they may fall as rain.

We can collect water from the air.

Fill a plastic bottle with water. Leave it in the fridge until it is really cold. Bring the bottle into a warm room. Look at the bottle after a few minutes.

Run your finger down the sides. What do you feel? The water vapour has become a **liquid** again.

CARRIED AWAY

Water runs from high ground down to seas and lakes.

When it **flows** it helps to shape the land. It can move heavy rocks. It can make **channels** in the soil.

Put some pebbles in a plastic tank.

Pour water slowly on to the pebbles.

What happens to them?

Pour the water faster. Does this make a difference?

Fill a large, deep tray with sand.

Rest one end on a book so that the tray slopes.

Gently pour water on to the sand at the top of the tray.

What happens to the water and the sand?

Rainwater fills our lakes, rivers and seas.
The gushing water has a lot of power to change the land.

SALTY OR FRESH

Water in the sea is salty. Water in streams and ponds is not salty and we call it fresh water. Many animals and plants that live in fresh water cannot live in salt water.

All plants and animals have water inside them.
Salty water draws out the water from some living things.

Feel two raw potato chips.

Taste a small piece of chip but don't swallow it. Does it taste salty or watery?

Snap one in half.
Does it break easily?

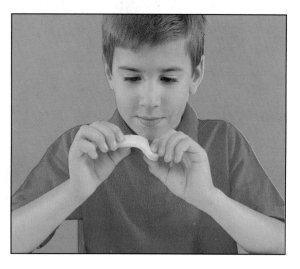

Put the other chip in a saucer. Sprinkle it with salt.

Watch what happens to the salt.
Leave it for half an hour.

How does it feel now?
Can you snap it in half?

The salt drew water out of the chip and made it bendy.

The animals and plants on the **coral reef** like the salty waters of the sea. They could not live in fresh water.

The water in the pond has turned to **ice**.
You can slide and skate on the slippery frozen water.

FREEZING COLD

When it gets very cold, water freezes.
It is cold to touch. It is **solid** but it can be **transparent.**

Half fill four plastic pots
with water.
Drop a handful of beads
in each.
Put the pots in the freezer.

When the water has
frozen, warm the pots a
little under the tap.
Slide the frozen water
and beads out into dishes.

Can you see the beads in
each pot to count them?

Find the quickest way to
reach them. Pour hot
water, salt, cold water
and sugar on to the ice.

Which melts it quickest?

Count the beads from
each pot in your hands.
Did you count right?

In some places, heat from inside the earth makes water
in the ground boil. It makes puddles of bubbling mud.

BOILING HOT

We use **boiling** water to cook foods.
Ask an adult to help you when you do any cooking.
Always take care with hot water. It can burn your skin.

Heat some water in a pan.

Watch it bubble when it is boiling hot. A water vapour called **steam** rises from the surface.

Crack an egg into a saucer.
Touch it. Look at its colour and shape.

Boil an egg for ten minutes.
Then let it cool down in cold water.

Crack the shell. Take out the egg and feel it.

Cut it in half.

How is it different from your raw egg?

TURN ON THE TAP

Most homes and buildings have a **water supply**.

Water runs through underground pipes from a **reservoir**. It fills the tanks in our homes.

The cold water tank stores the water.

Water in the hot tank is heated by electricity or by burning gas or oil in the **boiler**.

Hot and cold water runs in different pipes from the tanks to the taps.

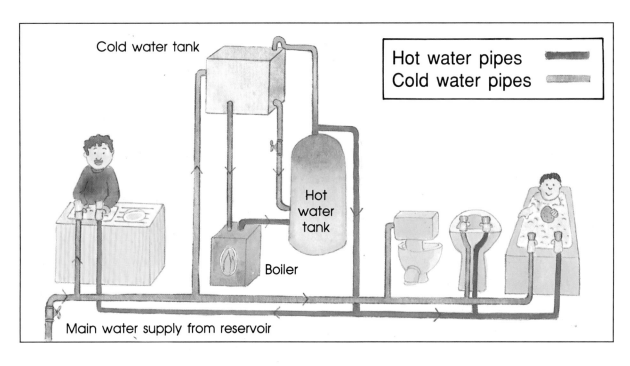

Cold water tank

Hot water pipes
Cold water pipes

Hot water tank

Boiler

Main water supply from reservoir

Draw a plan of your home. Draw in the water pipes from the tanks. Which rooms do they go to?

The water from the taps runs into the bath.
The bath is filled with a mixture of hot and cold water.

The sheets have been washed with washing powder.
The soapy water has made them really clean.

WASHING DAY

Make your hands really dirty with newspaper or cover them in paint.

Wash your hands in cold water. Can you get them really clean?
Now wash your hands in soapy water.
Are they cleaner now?

Can you get your hands cleaner with warm water?

Soap helps water get close to things like material.

Fill one jar with clean water and one with soapy water.
Cut two squares of the same size from a piece of material.
Float them on the top of each jar. Which square gets wet first?

The soapy water quickly fills the cloth and makes it wet.
Then the water can wash the dirt away easily.

SOAKING WET

Some materials can soak up water.
They **absorb** the water and become wet themselves.

Pour a cup of water on to
a tray.

Try to soak up the water
with a sheet of kitchen
paper.

Squeeze the paper into
an empty bowl.

How many squeezes do
you need to dry the tray?

Material	Number of squeezes
Paper towel	
Dish cloth	
Handkerchief	
Sponge	
Foil	
Polythene	

Test other materials too.

Try a paper towel, a dish
cloth, a handkerchief, a
sponge, some foil and
some polythene.

Record the number of
squeezes you have to use.

Does your chart show which materials absorb water
best? Do some materials absorb no water at all?

We get wet when we go swimming.
We can use a towel to dry the water from our skin.

DISAPPEARING TRICK

Some things **dissolve** in water.
When they dissolve, they disappear completely.
Hot or warm water can help them dissolve more quickly.

Half fill some jars with warm water.

Test lots of things to see if they dissolve.

Stir a teaspoon of each into separate jars.

Watch what happens.

Record your results like this:

	Dissolves	Becomes cloudy	Changes colour	Sinks	Floats
Sugar					
Sand					
Flour					
Soap powder					
Coffee					
Soil					
Salt					

Which things dissolve easily?
Are there some things that don't dissolve at all?

Some people take sugar in their tea.
The sugar **crystals** dissolve and can't be seen anymore.

The people know they will be safe if they fall in the water. Their life-jackets will keep them afloat.

BOATS AND FLOATS

Find a large **polystyrene** ceiling tile. Ask an adult to make a hole in the middle of it.

Float your tile in a tank of water.

Collect lots of small objects, such as pebbles, marbles, corks, grapes, crayons and buttons.

Stand them around the edge of the hole.

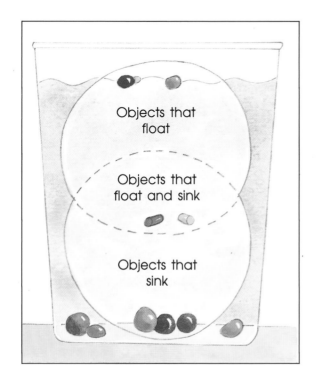

Objects that float

Objects that float and sink

Objects that sink

Guess if each object will float or sink before you push it into the water.

How many did you guess correctly?

Did any objects half sink and then stay floating in the middle of the tank?

Arrange your objects like this to show what they did.

WATER SPOUTS

Water is heavy. It always pushes down and tries to run or trickle away.

Rain-water tubs and watering cans hold water.

They have a tap or spout low down to let all the water out.

Can you think of any other water containers that work like this?

Make some holes down the side of an empty plastic bottle.

Cover the holes with sticky tape.

Fill the bottle with water.

Rip off the sticky tape.

What do you notice about the water coming from the holes?

The fun fountains shoot water high into the air.
Then the water falls back into the pool.

Even short grass has very long roots.
They reach down into the soil to take up water.

WET FEET

All plants need water to grow.

A plant gets its water from rain that collects in the soil.

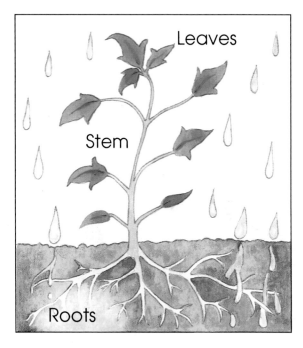

The water passes into the roots of the plant.

It travels up the stem and into the leaves.

Put a little water in a jug.

Stir a tablespoon of ink into the water.

Stand a stick of celery in the inky water.

Leave it for a day.

Take out the celery and cut through the stem.

Has the inky water passed up the stem?

27

There has been no rain and the river is dry.
The people have to dig down to find the water they need.

RUN DRY

Every living creature and plant needs water to live.

People use water many times every day.

Draw a 'water diary' for a day and keep a record of each time you use water.

My water diary

I watered my plant.

I gave my dog a drink.

I washed my hands.

I painted a picture.

I played with my toy boat.

How many things couldn't you do without water?

Could you clean your teeth? Could you wash your hair?

Think what would happen if you turned on the tap one day and no water came out.

GLOSSARY

Absorb Soak up.

Boiler A machine that heats up water.

Boiling When water is so hot it turns to steam.

Channels Passages that water runs along.

Coral reef The skeletons of dead and living sea creatures. They make rock-like shapes in the sea.

Crystals Solid, regular shapes like sugar and salt.

Dissolve When something solid is mixed with a liquid and disappears.

Flow To move smoothly like a liquid.

Gas A substance that is neither solid nor liquid. Air is made of gases.

Ice Frozen water.

Liquid A substance that is runny and can flow, like water.

Polystyrene A light, foamy substance.

Reservoir A place, like a lake, where water is collected and stored.

Solid Hard.

Steam The mixture of water vapour and water droplets. You can see it in the air when water boils.

Transparent See-through.

Water supply Water that runs in pipes direct to a building.

Water vapour A gas formed from water.

FINDING OUT MORE

Books to read:

Floating and Sinking by Kay Davies and Wendy Oldfield (Wayland, 1990)
Floating and Sinking by Henry Pluckrose (Franklin Watts, 1990)
My Boat by Kay Davies and Wendy Oldfield (A & C Black, 1990)
Waste by Kay Davies and Wendy Oldfield (Wayland, 1990)
Water by Bob Graham & Fay J. Humphreys (Blackie, 1988)
Water by Brenda Walpole (A & C Black, 1989)
Water by Angela Webb (Franklin Watts, 1990)

Teachers' resource:

The Southern Water Story (Southern Water, 1989) Pack containing six project cards, teachers' notes, safety booklet and reader. Available from Educational Projects Resources, Southern Water Education Service, FREEPOST, London SW7 4YY.

PICTURE ACKNOWLEDGEMENTS

Bruce Coleman Ltd, 26 (Crichton); Cephas Picture Library 25; Chapel Studios 15; Eye Ubiquitous 21, 28; J. Allan Cash 4; Tony Stone Worldwide 5 top, 7, 9; Wayland Picture Library 22, (Zul Mukhida) cover, 5 bottom, 6 both, 8 both, 11 both, 13 bottom, 17 bottom, 18, 20, 23, 24, 27; Tim Woodcock 13 top; ZEFA 10, 12, 16, 19.
Artwork illustrations by Rebecca Archer. The publishers would also like to thank the schools and children of Davigdor Infant's School and St. Andrews's C.E. School, both of Hove, East Sussex, and St. Bernadette's First & Middle School and Patcham House Day Special School, both of Brighton, East Sussex, for their kind co-operation.

INDEX

Page numbers in **bold** indicate subjects shown in pictures, but not mentioned in the text on those pages.